The NFL's Greatest Teams

TENNESSEE TITANS

Katie Lajiness

Big Buddy Books
An Imprint of Abdo Publishing
abdopublishing.com

abdopublishing.com

Published by Abdo Publishing, a division of ABDO, PO Box 398166, Minneapolis, Minnesota 55439.

Printed in the United States of America, North Mankato, Minnesota.
092016
012017

THIS BOOK CONTAINS RECYCLED MATERIALS

Cover Photo: ASSOCIATED PRESS.
Interior Photos: ASSOCIATED PRESS.

Coordinating Series Editor: Tamara L. Britton
Graphic Design: Michelle Labatt, Taylor Higgins, Jenny Christensen

Publisher's Cataloging-in-Publication Data

Names: Lajiness, Katie, author.
Title: Tennessee Titans / by Katie Lajiness.
Description: Minneapolis, MN : Abdo Publishing, 2017. | Series: NFL's greatest teams | Includes bibliographical references and index.
Identifiers: LCCN 2016944885 | ISBN 9781680785418 (lib. bdg.) | ISBN 9781680799019 (ebook)
Subjects: LCSH: Tennessee Titans (Football team)--History--Juvenile literature.
Classification: DDC 796.332--dc23
LC record available at http://lccn.loc.gov/2016944885

Contents

A Winning Team

The Tennessee Titans are a football team from Nashville, Tennessee. They have played in the National Football League (NFL) for more than 55 years.

The Titans have had good seasons and bad. But time and again, they've proven themselves. Let's see what makes the Titans one of the NFL's greatest teams.

Navy, light blue, and white are the team's colors.

League Play

The NFL got its start in 1920. Its teams have changed over the years. Today, there are 32 teams. They make up two conferences and eight divisions.

The Titans play in the South Division of the American Football Conference (AFC). This division also includes the Houston Texans, the Indianapolis Colts, and the Jacksonville Jaguars.

Team Standings

The AFC and the National Football Conference (NFC) make up the NFL. Each conference has a north, south, east, and west division.

The Jaguars are a major rival of the Titans. The teams have competed to be the best in their division.

Kicking Off

The team began play as the Houston Oilers. In 1960, they were based in Houston, Texas. The Oilers were one of the first teams in the American Football League (AFL).

At first, the Oilers were very successful. They won the AFL **championships** in 1960 and 1961! Both times they beat the San Diego Chargers.

George Blanda (16) was both a quarterback and a kicker.

Longest Game

In 1962, the Oilers lost to the Dallas Texans in the AFL championship. The game lasted 77 minutes and 54 seconds. At the time, it was the longest professional football game in history.

Highlight Reel

The AFL joined the NFL in 1970. For the next several years the Oilers struggled. But, in 1978 and 1979, the team made it to the conference **championship**. Sadly, the Oilers lost both games to the Pittsburgh Steelers.

The team saw success again starting in 1987. Quarterback Warren Moon led the team's powerful offense. And, they made it to the play-offs seven years in a row.

Win or Go Home

NFL teams play 16 regular season games each year. The teams with the best records are part of the play-off games. Play-off winners move on to the conference championships. Then, conference winners face off in the Super Bowl!

The 1979 championship game was played at Three Rivers Stadium in Pittsburgh, Pennsylvania.

In 1990, Warren Moon threw for 4,689 yards. This was a record at the time.

The late 1990s brought big changes for the team. In 1997, owner K.S. "Bud" Adams Jr. moved the team to Nashville. And, the team changed its name to the Tennessee Oilers.

The team's name changed again in 1999! The new name proved to be good luck. The Tennessee Titans won their first play-off game since 1993. And, the team played in its first Super Bowl!

In a 2000 play-off game, the Titans beat the Buffalo Bills. The Titans won in the final seconds of the game.

In 1997, Adams showed off the team logo. Over the years, the design changed many times.

Halftime! Stat Break

Team Records

RUSHING YARDS
Career: Eddie George, 10,009 yards (1996–2003)
Single Season: Chris Johnson, 2,006 yards (2009)
PASSING YARDS
Career: Warren Moon, 33,685 yards (1984–1993)
Single Season: Warren Moon, 4,690 yards (1991)
RECEPTIONS
Career: Ernest Givins, 542 receptions (1986–1994)
Single Season: Charley Hennigan, 101 receptions (1964)
ALL-TIME LEADING SCORER
Al Del Greco, 1,060 points (1991–2000)

Famous Coaches

Lou Rymkus (1960–1961)
Wally Lemm (1961, 1966–1970)
Jeff Fisher (1994–2010)

Championships

EARLY CHAMPIONSHIP WINS:
1960, 1961

SUPER BOWL APPEARANCES:
2000

SUPER BOWL WINS:
None

Fan Fun

STADIUM: Nissan Stadium
LOCATION: Nashville, Tennessee
MASCOT: T-Rac

Pro Football Hall of Famers & Their Years with the Titans

Elvin Bethea, Defensive End (1968–1983)
George Blanda, Quarterback/Kicker (1960–1966)
Earl Campbell, Running Back (1978–1984)
Curley Culp, Defensive Tackle (1974–1980)
Ken Houston, Strong Safety (1967–1972)
Bruce Matthews, Guard/Tackle/Center (1983–2001)
Warren Moon, Quarterback (1984–1993)
Mike Munchak, Guard (1982–1993)

Coaches' Corner

In 1960, Lou Rymkus was the first head coach of the Houston Oilers. He led the team to an 11–7 season and an AFL **championship** win. That year, Rymkus was named AFL Coach of the Year.

The next year, the Oilers got off to a bad season. Wally Lemm became head coach after Rymkus left the team. Under Lemm, the Oilers won the final nine games of the season. And, they won the AFL championship for the second time.

Rymkus coached the Titans from 1960 to 1961. He returned as the offensive line coach in 1965.

Lemm was honored with the AFL Coach of the Year award in 1961.

Star Players

George Blanda QUARTERBACK/KICKER (1960–1966)

In 1960, Blanda led the Oilers to the team's first AFL **championship**. The following year, the Oilers won the AFL championship again! And, Blanda was named the Most Valuable Player (MVP).

Elvin Bethea DEFENSIVE END (1968–1983)

Elvin Bethea played with the Oilers his entire **career**. When he **retired**, he held three team records. His first record was for most seasons played (16). He also holds a record for most career regular season games played (210). And, he played the most straight regular-season games in a row (135).

Curley Culp DEFENSIVE TACKLE (1974–1980)

Curley Culp came to the Oilers in a trade with the Kansas City Chiefs. In 1975, he had 11.5 sacks. Culp helped the Oilers to a winning season, which was their first in eight years. In 2013, he became a member of the Pro Football Hall of Fame.

Earl Campbell RUNNING BACK (1978–1984)

In 1978, Earl Campbell was the Oiler's first **draft** pick. In his **rookie** season, he was named MVP, Offensive Player of the Year, and Rookie of the Year! To honor him, the Titans no longer use number 34.

Mike Munchak GUARD (1982–1993)

In 1982, Mike Munchak was the team's first-round **draft** pick. Munchak and the team's offensive line led the NFL in total offense in 1990. He was selected to play in the Pro Bowl, which is the NFL's all-star game, nine times. Munchak played for the Oilers his entire **career**.

Bruce Matthews GUARD/TACKLE/CENTER (1983–2001)

The Oilers picked Bruce Matthews in the 1983 **draft**. He spent his entire **career** with the team. During that time he played in 296 NFL games. That was an NFL record! He was selected to play in the Pro Bowl 14 years in a row. This was another NFL record.

Warren Moon QUARTERBACK (1984–1993)

Warren Moon was one of the most successful quarterbacks in NFL history. He set many NFL passing records during his ten seasons with the Oilers. In 2006, Moon became the first African-American quarterback in the Pro Football Hall of Fame.

Nissan Stadium

The Titans play home games at Nissan Stadium. It is in Nashville. Nissan Stadium opened in 1999. It can hold more than 69,000 people.

Nissan Stadium was originally called Adelphia Coliseum.

The 12th Titan

Team Spirit

Football teams have 11 members on the field at a time. The fans are considered a twelfth member of the team.

The 12th Titan is a **tradition** at Nissan Stadium. At the start of each home game, a Titans fan is honored with a Sword of Honor. The fan can be a Tennessee celebrity, leader, hero, or a former Titans player.

T-Rac is the team's mascot. He rides his ATV before home games. Sometimes T-Rac drives it through a hoop!

The state animal of Tennessee is a raccoon.

Olympic gymnast Shawn Johnson holds a Sword of Honor at the 50-yard line.

Final Call

The Titans have a long, rich history. They won two early league **championships**. And, they played in the 2000 Super Bowl!

Even during losing seasons, true fans have stuck by them. Many believe the Tennessee Titans will remain one of the greatest teams in the NFL.

Titans fans show their team spirit by wearing fun hats!

The 2000 Super Bowl was held at the Georgia Dome in Atlanta, Georgia. More than 72,600 fans came to see the Titans play the Saint Louis Rams.

Through the Years

1960

The Houston Oilers play their first game as an AFL team.

1962

The team loses to the Dallas Texans in the AFL **championship**.

1968

The Oilers play in the NFL's first domed stadium.

1970

The AFL joins the NFL.

1981

Quarterback George Blanda is the first team player to become a member of the Pro Football Hall of Fame.

1990

Warren Moon is the first Oilers quarterback to pass for more than 4,000 yards in one season.

1997

The team moves to Nashville.

1999

T-Rac becomes the **mascot** of the Tennessee Titans.

2000

The Titans play in their first Super Bowl. They lose to the Saint Louis Rams 23–16.

2013

Owner Bud Adams Jr. dies. He was the longest owner of an NFL team.

Postgame Recap

1. What was the team's first name?
   A. Tennessee Oilers **B.** Houston Oilers **C.** Houston Titans

2. What year did the Titans play in the Super Bowl?
   A. 1999
   B. 2000
   C. 2001

3. Where is the team's stadium located?
   A. Chattanooga, Tennessee
   B. Knoxville, Tennessee
   C. Nashville, Tennessee

4. Name 3 of the 8 Titans in the Pro Football Hall of Fame.

1. B. 2. B. 3. C. 4. See page 15

Glossary

career a period of time spent in a certain job.

championship a game, a match, or a race held to find a first-place winner.

draft a system for professional sports teams to choose new players.

mascot something to bring good luck and help cheer on a team.

retire to give up one's job.

rookie a first-year player in a professional sport.

tradition (truh-DIH-shuhn) an inherited, established, or customary pattern of thought, action, or behavior.

Websites

To learn more about the NFL's Greatest Teams, visit **booklinks.abdopublishing.com**. These links are routinely monitored and updated to provide the most current information available.

Index